YOURS Sincerely

VALERIE EME ELYOTT

Independently published by Valerie Eme Elyott www.valeriee.online

First Published: July 2023

Illustrations by Ifrah Fatima and copyright © Valerie Eme Elyott

ISBN 9798852413888

DEDICATION

Thank You Holy Spirit for Your active presence in our lives. Thank You for never withholding what our hearts need. Life with You is everything!

18 reflective poems with commentary and scriptures, to help facilitate personal times of fellowship with the Lord.

CONTENTS

INTRODUCTION

Great conversations begin and end with all parties feeling heard. This is not always the case in our communication with the Lord. Sometimes we may feel unheard because we did not get an immediate response. At other times we are the ones rushing off and not listening to the Lord.

This book has been written to help facilitate some of those needed conversations with the Lord. It will cause you to reflect on truth and receive His perspective with clarity.

It is not intended for daily devotion, as each topic may take some time to process. It will help you 'guard your heart' as we are instructed to do in God's word.

The use of reflective poetry in this book is to give personally relatable perspectives, whilst encouraging sincerity of heart and transparency with the Lord. Some of the poems may resonate with you more than others, but still give the Lord a moment to share His heart with you concerning it.

Every verse of scripture has been prayerfully selected for purposeful meditation. Do not take them for granted as verses you already know. Meditate on them in the light of what the Lord is speaking to your heart in that moment.

As you read, reflect and pray, may you receive the Lord's wisdom, affirmation, correction and revelation as needed. He has a lot to say to you and wants to hear what you have to say too.

THE INVITATION

1
THE INVITATION

There are so many things
that My heart longs to share
secrets of My Kingdom
spoken for you to hear

My Spirit keeps on stirring
My desires in your heart
Do you hear the gentle whispers?
Will you do your own part?

My angels are ready
to move at my command
Some things I want to bring forth
by the power of My hand

This is your invitation
Come boldly to My throne
You are welcome in my presence
it is where you are fully known

YIELDING BY FAITH

2
YIELDING BY FAITH

Is it worth trying to hide from God
what He already knows?
I will give in to faith
and just see how this goes

He sees my heart, knows my thoughts
and knows just where to start
Lord, here I am once again
and this time, here is my whole heart

"¹O Lᴏʀᴅ, you have searched me [thoroughly] and have known me.
² You know when I sit down and when I rise up [my entire life, everything I do];
You understand my thought from afar.
³ You scrutinize my path and my lying down,
And You are intimately acquainted with all my ways.
⁴ Even before there is a word on my tongue [still unspoken],
Behold, O Lᴏʀᴅ, You know it all."
- Psalm 139:1-4 Amplified Bible

"Nothing in all creation is hidden from God. Everything is naked and exposed before his eyes, and he is the one to whom we are accountable."
- Hebrews 4:13, New Living Translation

I love how relevant and applicable the scriptures are to our daily lives. The verses above remind us how all-knowing our heavenly Father is. There is nothing He does not know, cannot know or has not known. There is nothing that could ever be hidden from Him. He sees it all, knows it all and loves us all the same.

This is why pretense with Him is futile. Though we may have mastered our skills of pretense and deception, we cannot deceive the Lord. He truly sees it all, knows it all and still draws us to Himself. This makes the unconditional nature of His love irrefutable.

THERE IS NOTHING IN YOUR LIFE THAT IS TOO BIG, TOO BAD OR TOO COMPLICATED FOR THE LORD.

"Why would He love me this way?" you might ask.

He might respond to you saying:

"I love you completely, never partially. I considered every part of you, every side of you, before I said the very first 'I love you!'

I put a plan in place for moments of fear, guilt, shame and doubt. My word gives guidance for vulnerable moments like these;

For we do not have a High Priest who is unable to sympathize and understand our weaknesses and temptations, but One who has been tempted [knowing exactly how it feels to be human] in every respect as we are, yet without [committing any] sin. [16] Therefore let us [with privilege] approach the throne of grace [that is, the throne of God's gracious favor] with confidence and without fear, so that we may receive mercy [for our failures] and find [His amazing] grace to help in time of need [an appropriate blessing, coming just at the right moment].
- Hebrews 4:15-16, Amplified Bible

So, draw near. Do not hold back in fear or shame. My grace is available to you. My mercy embraces you. My power is at work right now concerning you. You are safe, my child. You are safe right here with Me."

How would you respond to that?

PAUSE:

Take some time now to think about your response.

- What would drawing nearer to Jesus look like in the context of your own life?

- How can you put it into action?

MEDITATE:

Proverbs 28:13 Amplified Bible
"He who conceals his transgressions will not prosper,
But whoever confesses and turns away from his
sins will find compassion and mercy."

Psalm 32:5, The Message
"Then I let it all out; I said, "I'll come clean about my
failures to God." Suddenly the pressure was gone, my
guilt dissolved, my sin disappeared."

James 4:6-8
But He gives us more and more grace [through
the power of the Holy Spirit to defy sin and live an
obedient life that reflects both our faith and our
gratitude for our salvation]. Therefore, it says,
"GOD IS OPPOSED TO THE PROUD and HAUGHTY, BUT
[continually] GIVES [the gift of] GRACE TO THE HUMBLE
[who turn away from self-righteousness]." So submit
to [the authority of] God. Resist the devil [stand firm
against him] and he will flee from you. Come close to
God [with a contrite heart] and He will come close to
you. Wash your hands, you sinners; and purify your
[unfaithful] hearts, you double-minded [people].

KEEPING FOCUS

3
KEEPING FOCUS

Here I am, Lord.
I have chosen to draw near
Yielding to Your voice
and willing to hear

I sense my mind reaching
for its own fleshly need
which is getting things done
with a whole lot of speed

Please help me to be present
Here is my full attention
Help me to embrace this moment
No calls, no clicks, no interruptions

No rushing through my prayers
and wanting to be done
No trying to be phony
before the Holy one

We've been here before
but this time it is different
Here I am, Lord
Please make this time well spent

We now live in a world that seems to demand our undivided attention for everything happening around us, at every point in time; be it virtually or physically. Whilst we may think that we have mastered the art of multi-tasking, we may have actually suppressed our innate ability to focus. This has become so normal to us that we cannot tell the difference between a distraction and multi-tasking.

This issue transcends our activities and interactions. It affects the way that our minds work. We take pride in the juggling acts we call productivity, without considering the negative impact it has on other things.

Taking one's time is seen as being slow. Speed is now considered efficiency, but at what cost? As great as it is to move quickly through tasks, relating to people does not work the same way. We are using less words to communicate important information. Images, emojis and abbreviations are used to sum up full sentences.

This may be a fun way of communicating and is appropriate for certain contexts, but relationships suffer if communication and interactions are done in the quickest and easiest ways possible.

Our relationship with the Lord and our times of communing with Him are of the highest priority for a Christian. There are no abbreviations for scripture and no magic button for connecting to the presence of God. It requires our whole heart and our full attention.

Lingering in His presence is becoming less common in church services or fellowship gatherings. We want efficient services, meaning short and sweet, so we can move on to the next thing. We seem to forget that spending time with the Lord is for our own benefit, not His. We are not doing the Lord any favours by praying, going to church or reading the bible. It is all for our own benefit and is actually our spiritual sustenance. He is already God. We cannot do anything to make Him any more or less the God of all creation.

Although our Lord Jesus Christ fulfilled the law on our behalf, there is still one commandment that remains ours to keep as part of our personal relationship with God. This particular commandment cannot be fulfilled on behalf of another because of the nature of relationships.

In this restored relationship with our heavenly Father, we have to be active participants. We are not being asked to bring anything to the table except our presence, our faith and our yielded hearts. Everything has been laid out for us. The law is no longer the way to earn righteousness, but now the principles that reveal God's standard for our lives.

This commandment quoted in Matthew 22:36-38 is one that remains relevant to maintaining a life of fellowship with the Lord, even in this dispensation of grace.

"Teacher, which is the greatest commandment in the Law?" And Jesus replied to him, 'YOU SHALL LOVE THE LORD YOUR GOD WITH ALL YOUR HEART, AND WITH ALL YOUR SOUL, AND WITH ALL YOUR MIND.' This is the first and greatest commandment.
- Matthew 22:36-38, Amplified Bible

The Lord Jesus Himself cannot do this for any of us because it is all about getting intimately personal with God. Loving God is not about our feelings for Him, but our actions being in accordance with His word. Love from God's perspective means to keep His commandments.

"If you [really] love Me, you will keep and obey My commandments.
- John 14:15-31, Amplified Bible

When we keep something, we are mindful of it. We care about it and want the owner to be pleased with how we handle it. Our honour of His word and His ways are expressions of our love for Him. It is more than 'obeying', simply doing because it is expected of you. It is caring about what you are doing and whose instruction you are following. This is the only way that He receives our Love.

His love for us is settled. The sacrifice of Jesus settled it once and for all. It is perfect, unlimited and unrivalled. His love protects us, heals us, fills us, corrects us, strengthens us and transforms us.

THERE IS NO SHORTCUT TO WALKING WITH GOD. SPIRITUAL GROWTH TAKES AS LONG AS IT TAKES FOR EVERY SINGLE ONE OF US. IT IS A LIFELONG PROCESS.

Make the most of the access you have been given to the King of kings. Make Him your focal point.

PAUSE:

What can you do to improve your concentration during your times of fellowship with the Lord?

What would it look like for you to love the Lord with:

- all of your heart

- all of your soul

- all of your mind?

MEDITATE:

Psalm 145:18, New Living Translation
The LORD is close to all who call on him, yes, to all who call on him in truth.

Psalm 19:14, New Living Translation
May the words of my mouth and the meditation of my heart be pleasing to you, O LORD, my rock and my redeemer.

Ephesians 5:15-16, Amplified Bible
Therefore see that you walk carefully [living life with honor, purpose, and courage; shunning those who tolerate and enable evil], not as the unwise, but as wise [sensible, intelligent, discerning people], making the very most of your time [on earth, recognizing and taking advantage of each opportunity and using it with wisdom and diligence], because the days are [filled with] evil.

THE BLAME GAME

4
THE BLAME GAME

I know whose fault this is
but I will not say the name
I refuse to be silent
and take all of the blame

It never would have happened
if they did not force my hand
Why me? Why now?
And why this reprimand?

"It was not my fault!"
"They made me do it!"
"This is so unfair!"

These claims are likely to be heard from a sulking child or an adult refusing to take responsibility for their actions.

In life, we will all be wronged and we will do wrong. There are times that we may not initiate the wrongdoing but our response to it may be just as wrong. Times like these call for God's grace and correction. As children of God, He parents us by teaching, guiding, providing for us and protecting us. He also proves His love for us with correction and discipline when it is needed. This is confirmed in the scriptures:

"But you have forgotten that the Scriptures say to God's children, "When the Lord punishes you, don't make light of it, and when he corrects you, don't be discouraged. The Lord corrects the people he loves and disciplines those he calls his own."

Be patient when you are being corrected! This is how God treats his children. Don't all parents correct their children? God corrects all his children, and if he doesn't correct you, then you don't really belong to him. Our earthly fathers correct us, and we still respect them. Isn't it even better to be given true life by letting our spiritual Father correct us? Our human fathers correct us for a short time, and they do it as they think best. But God corrects us for our own good, because he wants us to be holy, as he is. It is never fun to be corrected.

In fact, at the time it is always painful. But if we learn to obey by being corrected, we will do right and live at peace.
– Hebrews 12:5-11, Contemporary English Version

It is an expression of God's unfailing love when He corrects us because His corrections keep us in alignment with our true nature and godly character. He protects us from destruction and the evil consequences that follow sin. Correction and discipline may be uncomfortable or painful in that moment but it results in a safer, more godly and fruitful life.

Taking responsibility for our actions is a big part of growing up. It is an important part of our mental, emotional and spiritual growth. It is a sign of maturity and also an expression of contrition.

When we refuse to admit our wrong and accept the consequences of our actions, we are actually rejecting an opportunity to receive God's mercy, wisdom and even justice.

Playing the victim with the Lord is never a wise thing to do, especially when we know that we are guilty of all or some of the wrong done. We must remember that He sees the full picture at all times and knows all the details better than we ever would. He is always willing to hear us out and will give us His counsel. We just have to be willing to receive it and be sensitive to His heart concerning the matter.

HIS MERCY IS ALWAYS EXTENDED TO US BUT ONLY THOSE HUMBLE ENOUGH TO ACKNOWLEDGE THEIR NEED OF IT, RECEIVE IT.

Also, remember that victims cry out for help and justice, not mercy and forgiveness. Could it be that you have been crying out for the wrong thing? Think about that for a moment.

What is needed for growth in one life is sometimes different from what is needed for growth in another life. Therefore, what is considered to be unfair for one person, may be the same thing needed as a growth opportunity for another. The Lord knows who we are, what we need and how to train us accordingly.

You can rest assured that the Lord sees your distress and knows just what you need. He is the God who protects and defends you. He the God who sees you.

PAUSE:

Is there any unresolved situation that has come to mind?

Look at it again from the Lord's perspective. Ask Him to show you how He sees it.

What is the Lord saying to you about it?

What is your response?

Who should you offer mercy and forgiveness to today?

MEDITATE:

Matthew 6:12, New Living Translation
"and forgive us our sins, as we have forgiven those who sin against us."

Romans 12:17-18, New Living Translation
Never pay back evil with more evil. Do things in such a way that everyone can see you are honorable. Do all that you can to live in peace with everyone.

Colossians 3:12-13, Amplified Bible
So, as God's own chosen people, who are holy [set apart, sanctified for His purpose] and well-beloved [by God Himself], put on a heart of compassion, kindness, humility, gentleness, and patience [which has the power to endure whatever injustice or unpleasantness comes, with good temper]; bearing graciously with one another, and willingly forgiving each other if one has a cause for complaint against another; just as the Lord has forgiven you, so should you forgive.

GROWING UP!

5
GROWING UP!

You said that it was okay
and now you say it's not!
This process of spiritual growth
is deeper than I thought

I now realize that there is always
something new to learn
You are helping me to mature
I see it clearer now, than then

The one thing that is certain about growth is change. As human beings our growth is usually measured by height, weight and intellectual ability, while as spiritual people, our growth is measured by capacity, depth and corresponding activity; which has to do with measure, fullness and obedience.

Our spiritual capacity determines how much we can receive or handle, our spiritual depth quantifies how much revelation has been received and our corresponding activity confirms our submission to the counsel of God by implementing revelations received. Since our God is limitless and we as created beings are not, we will continue to learn something new and conform to His truth as we develop in our relationship with Him.

JUST WHEN WE THINK WE HAVE MASTERED SOMETHING, WE ARE INTRODUCED TO ANOTHER LAYER OF TRUTH ABOUT THE SAME THING.

This is the reality of life in Christ. Although we have been given a new heart, we are always surrounded by contradictory influences. This is why we are regularly refined and pruned by our heavenly Father, who knows us perfectly and sees us in the fullness of truth. He continues to stir our hearts and draw us into the reality of all that He knows us to be in Him, with every instruction for change.

Change, as unwelcome as it often is, presents us with new opportunities to personally experience life in Christ in much deeper and more powerful ways.

If 'Change' could speak, here is what you might hear:

Hello!

Yes, it's me again.
The unscheduled but regular guest in your life.
The one that surprised you at your birth.
The one that is present with you in every 'new'.
The one always on the other side of growth, calling you in.
The one you often reluctantly embrace.

I present you with both challenges and opportunities.
I am often the reason for a before and an after.
I have been an easy excuse for endings
and a great one for new beginnings.
I will always be around, in one expression or another.

*You call me **Change**.*

Around the world I am known to be the same,
although the reason I exist is to make a difference.
I bring you into the new by drawing you out of the old.
I am the former enemy that becomes the new best friend.
My impact is felt, no matter how little or great.
Each moment with me guarantees a new experience.
I am occasionally the 'welcome unfamiliar'.
Definitely needed but often not wanted.

Here is my personal disclaimer:

- *It is not entirely up to me if everything works out.*

- *As powerful as I seem to be, I am actually just an expression of spiritual, physical, emotional, intellectual or environmental activity.*

- *When I come knocking, it is a signal for your attention. Something old is done and something new is coming!*

- *It is wise to prepare for my arrival, although I sometimes show up unannounced.*

- *I have no power of my own, except for what is attributed to me. The real power is in your reactions or responses to your awareness of me.*

- *I expect you to take the time to know what you need to know, do what you need to do correctly, consistently and to the best of your ability, to get the best out of me.*

So, please do not resist me anymore. Stop pushing me away or keeping me waiting. Ignoring me only delays your progress.

I could be your friend.
The one you never knew you needed.

Yours always,

Change.

PAUSE:

Have you recognised God's orchestrated changes in your life?

How have you responded to them?

What would another level of maturity look like in your life?

MEDITATE:

1 Corinthians 13:11, Amplified Bible Classic Edition
When I was a child, I talked like a child, I thought like a child, I reasoned like a child; now that I have become a man, I am done with childish ways and have put them aside.

Isaiah 43:18-19, Amplified Bible
"Do not remember the former things, or ponder the things of the past. Listen carefully, I am about to do a new thing, Now it will spring forth; Will you not be aware of it? I will even put a road in the wilderness, Rivers in the desert".

Luke 2:52, Amplified Bible
And Jesus kept increasing in wisdom and in stature, and in favor with God and men.

SORRY, NOT SORRY!

6
SORRY, NOT SORRY!

I said I was sorry
but I know that I was not
I owned up and came clean
before I could get caught

It weighed on me heavily
and messed with my sleep
That secret was quite troubling,
It was not one to keep

With all that off my chest
I move on to other things
I do my declarations
shout them out and even sing

I never skip devotion
and always pray for long
So, why am I still troubled?
Have I got it all wrong?

I once shared a message called Sweet Confessions. The title was very intriguing but it was not about juicy secrets being revealed. It was a devotional message that led listeners into a reflective moment of truth about confession and repentance. It was a message about the sincerity of our words and actions.

Confession in the context of this chapter, is an acknowledgement or declaration of guilt, which involves the use of words; spoken, written or signed.

There is something about talking or sharing with someone that makes us feel better about ourselves or our situations. We share to express, we share to reveal and we share to release. More so with confession. I guess that's why there is the saying that, 'Confession is good for the soul'.

Most parents know when their children are telling the truth. They can usually tell if a confession is sincere and remorseful. They can tell if the child is just getting it off their chest, doing some damage control or having an 'oops!' moment. The truth is revealed through actions over time. In an even more accurate and detailed way, our heavenly Father always knows the truth concerning us. Not our truth, but the only truth there is. God's truth considers all sides of the story and nothing is hidden from Him. He knows our hearts better than we ever would and knows how to help us align with His will.

Repentance on the other hand, in my simple description, is rejecting what is wrong to accept to what is right. It is deciding in your heart to turn away from what you know to be wrong and embracing what is right. Whilst confession is all about communication, repentance is about actions. A repentant confession would involve words and actions. Speaking truthfully and remorsefully, with corresponding actions to follow. Speaking about it and turning from it at the same time.

CONFESSION IS NOT NECESSARILY REPENTANCE AND REPENTANCE MAY NOT INCLUDE CONFESSION.

It is important to differentiate between the two because they are often confused as being the same thing. Since confession is about communicating something, it can be done without any sense of regret or a change of heart. It might just be a verbal acknowledgment of a wrong done. Casually owning up to it but not owning it! Saying "I did it" but not taking any responsibility for the related consequences. It could simply just be what I call a 'sweet confession'. Getting it off your chest or even bragging about it. It is not necessarily about feeling apologetic for the wrong done and wanting change.

Repentance is more than spoken words. Though the decision may be communicated, it is confirmed through corresponding action. It produces a change for the better. Godly confession is not without repentance.

The last two verses of that poem describe what some Christians take for granted. Prayers and worship from an unrepentant heart are unacceptable to the Lord. Pretending to be repentant and confessing insincerely is actually an act of dishonour to the Lord because He cannot be deceived. I like how this scripture says it:

"Do not be deceived *and* deluded *and* misled; God will not allow Himself to be sneered at (scorned, disdained, or mocked by mere pretensions or professions, or by His precepts being set aside.) [He inevitably deludes himself who attempts to delude God.] For whatever a man sows, that *and* that only is what he will reap".
- Galatians 6:7, Amplified Bible Classic Edition

We may be able to deceive others, but we can never deceive God.

PAUSE:

Take a moment to pray about any issues that came to mind as you were reading that.

Practice true confession with the Lord right now.

What would repentance look like in those situations?

What is the Lord saying to you right now?

MEDITATE:

Acts 3:19 Amplified Bible
So repent [change your inner self—your old way of thinking, regret past sins] and return [to God—seek His purpose for your life], so that your sins may be wiped away [blotted out, completely erased], so that times of refreshing may come from the presence of the Lord [restoring you like a cool wind on a hot day];

Matthew 3:8, Amplified Bible
So produce fruit that is consistent with repentance [demonstrating new behavior that proves a change of heart, and a conscious decision to turn away from sin];

Proverbs 28:13, Amplified Bible
He who conceals his transgressions will not prosper, but whoever confesses and turns away from his sins will find compassion *and* mercy.

Ephesians 4:25. Amplified Bible
Therefore, rejecting all falsehood [whether lying, defrauding, telling half-truths, spreading rumors, any such as these], SPEAK TRUTH EACH ONE WITH HIS NEIGHBOR, for we are all parts of one another [and we are all parts of the body of Christ].

NO MORE EMPTY WORDS!

7
NO MORE EMPTY WORDS!

I use my words however I choose
not giving them much thought
As long as it is what needs to be heard
whether it is true or not

I speak this way with everyone
and sometimes with You, Lord
This needs to stop. I need your help
Please show me the way forward

No word is empty. Everything we say has a meaning whether it is considered or not. For fear of rejection or offending others, we sometimes say whatever seems acceptable in the moment, even if it is not true. It is usually considered a harmless lie. These words, though harmless to the speaker may be harmful to the hearer or impact their circumstances negatively.

Thoughtless communications are just as bad when done in excitement, as they are when done in anger. Promises made when emotions override thought and reason are usually very costly or will never be fulfilled. A 'Yes!' is more than a word for expressing agreeability, when actual expectations are attached to it.

EVERY WORD COMMUNICATES SOMETHING AND EVERY WORD CARRIES THE VALUE OF ITS MEANING, WHETHER IT IS SPOKEN TRUTHFULLY OR NOT.

When we speak thoughtlessly in anger, we cause damage that may be irreparable. We sometimes say the most hurtful things because of how we feel in that moment, but when the moment passes, the impact of the words remain and the consequences follow. "I did not mean it!" or "I was only joking." would not suffice.

In the book of John, our Lord Jesus is called the Word of God. In Colossians, He is the visible image of the invisible God. He is the full expression of our heavenly Father's heart to creation. Our Lord Jesus, is God's perfect communication to humanity.

Since we are made in the likeness of God and His words manifest their meaning, we should value our ability to speak and the power in our words. They bring forth the meaning and intent of that which is spoken. This must not be taken lightly, as the bible says "The tongue can bring death or life; those who love to talk will reap the consequences."
- Proverbs 18:21, New Living Translation

The solution to not saying anything damaging, is not only saying nice things. The solution is speaking with mindful consideration. Besides, saying nice things just to gain an advantage is unacceptable to the Lord. I love that the Bible has something to say about this seemingly harmless act of insincere kindness through words, called flattery.

A lying tongue hates those it wounds *and* crushes, And a flattering mouth works ruin.
- Proverbs 26:28, Amplified Bible

They speak deceitful *and* worthless words to one another; with flattering lips and a double heart they speak.
- Psalm 12:2, Amplified Bible

When flattery is spoken, it is not for the benefit of the one being spoken to. It is a very selfish act. This is why it is considered in the same category as lying and deceitfulness. Yet, this is deemed acceptable and harmless by many Christians.

Why does this matter? There are many other worse things to consider a sin, so why would this matter at all? Well, it matters because it is has to do with the motive of our hearts. To give a compliment or praise with the aim of manipulating a person or situation is deceitful. The words may be true but the motive is wrong. While people listen to our words, the Lord listens to our hearts. The Lord measures the truth of our words by the motive of our hearts, not by factual accuracy.

This matters since we are made in the likeness of God. We must handle words like He does. He has no empty words, and neither do we. According to this verse, "The words *and* promises of the LORD are pure words, like silver refined in an earthen furnace, purified seven times."
- Psalm 12:6, Amplified Bible

Our words are powerful. Our words create. The purity of our words are valued by the motive of our hearts. Before God, our words are a reflection of who we are and reveal the true state of our hearts.

May the Lord help us value our words as vessels of life and power that create what is spoken, and in our speaking, may the motive of our hearts be pure before the Lord. Amen.

PAUSE:

Take a moment to appreciate the value of words to God.

How have you handled your words?

What would you like to say to the Lord about this?

What is He saying to you in response?

MEDITATE:

Ecclesiastes 5:2, Amplified Bible

[2] Do not be hasty with your mouth [speaking careless words or vows] or impulsive in thought to bring up a matter before God. For God is in heaven and you are on earth; therefore let your words be few.

Ecclesiastes 5:4-5, New Living Translation

[4] When you make a promise to God, don't delay in following through, for God takes no pleasure in fools. Keep all the promises you make to him. [5] It is better to say nothing than to make a promise and not keep it.

Matthew 12:36, Amplified Bible

[36] But I tell you, on the day of judgment people will have to give an accounting for every careless *or* useless word they speak.

Colossians 3:8-10, Amplified Bible

[8] But now rid yourselves [completely] of all these things: anger, rage, malice, slander, and obscene (abusive, filthy, vulgar) language from your mouth. [9] Do not lie to one another, for you have stripped off the old self with its *evil* practices, [10] and have put on the new [spiritual] self who is being *continually* renewed in true knowledge in the image of Him who created the new self.

IT WAS NOT ME!

8
IT WAS NOT ME!

The fear of being rejected
is why I have not shared
If I must be honest
I have never really dared
To speak up for myself
and make my voice heard
I'm not the one who did the wrong
so why am I so scared?

One day David asked, "Is anyone in Saul's family still alive—anyone to whom I can show kindness for Jonathan's sake?" ² He summoned a man named Ziba, who had been one of Saul's servants. "Are you Ziba?" the king asked.

"Yes sir, I am," Ziba replied.

The king then asked him, "Is anyone still alive from Saul's family? If so, I want to show God's kindness to them."

Ziba replied, "Yes, one of Jonathan's sons is still alive. He is crippled in both feet."

"Where is he?" the king asked.

"In Lo-debar," Ziba told him, "at the home of Makir son of Ammiel."

So David sent for him and brought him from Makir's home. His name was Mephibosheth; he was Jonathan's son and Saul's grandson. When he came to David, he bowed low to the ground in deep respect. David said, "Greetings, Mephibosheth."

Mephibosheth replied, "I am your servant."

"Don't be afraid!" David said. "I intend to show kindness to you because of my promise to your father, Jonathan. I will give you all the property that once belonged to your grandfather Saul, and you will eat here with me at the king's table!"

Mephibosheth bowed respectfully and exclaimed, "Who is your servant, that you should show such kindness to a dead dog like me?" Then the king summoned Saul's servant Ziba and said, "I have given your master's grandson everything that belonged to Saul and his family. You and your sons and servants are to farm the land for him to produce food for your master's household. But Mephibosheth, your master's grandson, will eat here at my table." (Ziba had fifteen sons and twenty servants.)

Ziba replied, "Yes, my lord the king; I am your servant, and I will do all that you have commanded." And from that time on, Mephibosheth ate regularly at David's table, like one of the king's own sons.

Mephibosheth had a young son named Mica. From then on, all the members of Ziba's household were Mephibosheth's servants. And Mephibosheth, who was crippled in both feet, lived in Jerusalem and ate regularly at the king's table. - 2 Samuel 9, New Living Translation

This story always touches a deep place in my heart. Such love! Such kindness! Such mercy! Such favour! Such faithfulness of God!

Mephibosheth suffered many wrongs and also lived in fear. He lived in fear of what the truth revealed would cause in his life. According to the bible, he was King Saul's grandson, Jonathan's son. Had David never been crowned king he would probably be in line for the throne. Yet the shame of his physical handicap and the fear of his secret being exposed was a daily reality. He had valid reasons to live in fear for his life, as he would have been considered an enemy of the reigning king because of his linage.

There are certain times in life that we go through some very terrible situations at the hands or by the making of others.

These situations may position us as victims and helpless ones, but we are too afraid to ask for help or speak up.

What usually stops us in these situations is the fear of what might happen. What would the consequences be? Would they believe you? Would they blame you? Would you be punished instead?

You may have given up hope of any help and like Mephibosheth, you may have found your peace and safety in hiding. Well, whatever your case may be, you need to remember that it was not your fault. The horrible things that you experienced through others, was not your fault.

Even if you were blamed for it, the Lord is reminding you right now that you are not to blame for what happened to you. This matters because except you see it differently and remember it correctly, you will remain in the guilt and shame of it forever. The Lord wants you free and whole again and this is possible with Him.

Mephibosheth's story shows how the kindness and faith-fulness of the Lord can restore our lives. He may never have walked again as a permanent scar of his suffering, but he lived the rest of his life in the reality of a life he once knew and was ordained to live.

IT DOES NOT MATTER HOW HIDDEN OR SILENT YOU HAVE BEEN OVER THE YEARS, THE LORD SEES YOU AND HEARS YOU VERY CLEARLY.

As the Lord did for Mephibosheth, He can do for you. Open up and share your heart with Him. Do not draw back in fear, guilt or shame. The Lord already knows about it, but He would love to hear it all from you.

PAUSE:

Go ahead and share your heart with the Lord. What happened to you?

What practical steps can you take to receive the help you need for your recovery or restoration?

What would restoration look like in your life? Ask the Lord to show you from His perspective.

MEDITATE:

Romans 8:35, 37-39, New Living Translation
Can anything ever separate us from Christ's love? Does it mean he no longer loves us if we have trouble or calamity, or are persecuted, or hungry, or destitute, or in danger, or threatened with death?

No, despite all these things, overwhelming victory is ours through Christ, who loved us.

And I am convinced that nothing can ever separate us from God's love. Neither death nor life, neither angels nor demons, neither our fears for today nor our worries about tomorrow—not even the powers of hell can separate us from God's love. No power in the sky above or in the earth below—indeed, nothing in all creation will ever be able to separate us from the love of God that is revealed in Christ Jesus our Lord.

Isaiah 43:1-4, MSG
But now, God's Message, the God who made you in the first place, Jacob, the One who got you started, Israel: "Don't be afraid, I've redeemed you. I've called your name. You're mine. When you're in over your head, I'll be there with you. When you're in rough waters, you will not go down. When you're between a rock and a hard place, it won't be a dead end— Because I

am God, your personal God, The Holy of Israel, your Savior. I paid a huge price for you: all of Egypt, with rich Cush and Seba thrown in! *That's* how much you mean to me! *That's* how much I love you! I'd sell off the whole world to get you back, trade the creation just for you.

VOICE OF MY HEART

9
VOICE OF MY HEART

You hear it loud and clear
although my lips are sealed
My words keep pouring out
my soul refuses to be stilled

This is a conversation
I am trying not to have
Despite keeping my mouth shut
it's being done on my behalf

This is the way you hear me
You listen to my heart
You know my every motive
and hear me before I start

I don't want to get used to
keeping it all locked up in here
Please help me, Lord. We need to talk
I have so much to share!

One of my favourite hymns from childhood always reminds me about the tender heart of the Lord for me. It affirms my heart about His perfect love and friendship extended to me.

"What a Friend we have in Jesus,
all our sins and griefs to bear!
What a privilege to carry
everything to God in prayer!
O what peace we often forfeit,
O what needless pain we bear,
All because we do not carry
everything to God in prayer." [1]

Such a powerful reminder to simply pray. Prayer most times is done as a monologue, although it is meant to be a dialogue. A heartfelt conversation between two listening friends.

We have been invited into a multifaceted relationship with the Lord, as our Lord, Saviour, King, Teacher, Leader, Brother and Friend, amongst other things. In John 15, our Lord Jesus brought His disciples into another level of relationship when He called them friends and no longer servants.

He was teaching them that relationship with Him was not just about working together or serving Him, but also very much about companionship. Belonging together.

[1] What a Friend We Have in Jesus - Witten by Charles Crozat Converse / Paul Joseph Baloche / Joseph Medlicott Scriven

This applies to us too. As His disciples, the Lord extends this invitation of friendship to us. We can trust Him because He has already proven Himself as the perfect friend. As one who lays down His life for us, granting us an audience with Him anytime.

Friendship is a two-way street. The Lord's offer must be reciprocated by us for this friendship to be established. We are to lay down our lives for Him daily and care about what He cares about. Very importantly, friends make the time to connect and share with one another. This is something that the Lord has fulfilled and continues to on a daily basis. He has given us His written word as steady access to the knowledge of His ways and given us the Holy Spirit to keep us in oneness with Him. He is willing to speak and listen to us at any time. The question is, how available are we for this friendship? Are we too busy serving Him and living our lives to make the time to connect with Him beyond bringing a prayer list?

GREAT RELATIONSHIPS ARE NOT FORCED. THEY ARE CULTIVATED AND NURTURED BY INVESTING TIME, HONESTY AND CARE.

The Lord truly cares for us. He cares about all that concerns us and wants to be actively included in our daily lives. He knows us better than we would ever know ourselves or what we are really in need of. He knows how to meet our needs and will surely surpass our greatest expectations. This is why we should not hold back from expressing our hearts to Him.

David, who was known as a man after the Lord's heart, knew this well and expressed it so beautifully in one of his psalms.

"God, I invite your searching gaze into my heart.
Examine me through and through;
find out everything that may be hidden within me.
Put me to the test and sift through all my anxious cares.
See if there is any path of pain I'm walking on,
and lead me back to your glorious, everlasting way—
the path that brings me back to you."
- Psalms 139:23-24 - TPT

I encourage you to follow David's example. Be confident in the Lord's perfect knowledge of you and be vulnerable with Him.

PAUSE:

What is on your heart? What have you not shared with the Lord in detail? He knows it already but there is something special about when you share it willingly with Him.

Do you have candid moments of friendship with the Lord?

What can you do differently to cultivate that in your life?

MEDITATE:

John 15:13-15, New Living Translation
There is no greater love than to lay down one's life for one's friends. You are my friends if you do what I command. I no longer call you slaves, because a master doesn't confide in his slaves. Now you are my friends, since I have told you everything the Father told me.

1 Peter 5:7, Amplified Bible
casting all your cares [all your anxieties, all your worries, and all your concerns, once and for all] on Him, for He cares about you [with deepest affection, and watches over you very carefully].

Matthew 6:25, Amplified Bible
"Therefore I tell you, stop being worried *or* anxious (perpetually uneasy, distracted) about your life, as to what you will eat or what you will drink; nor about your body, as to what you will wear. Is life not more than food, and the body more than clothing?

LOVING ME

10
LOVING ME

I sometimes struggle to believe
that You love me this much
I think of where you found me
And the power of Your touch

I know You do not lie, Lord
But sometimes I feel you're wrong
The things you say about me
Sound just like a love song

I am still learning to surrender
I mess up a lot of times
Yet you hold me closely
And say "You are still mine."

Please help my heart to get it
To know that this is real
This is Your truth about me
No matter how I feel

Awe and wonder is a common response to the incredibility of salvation. Not only are we loved and chosen, but we are also known in our individuality even as we are known as one people. The body of Christ.

There is something about understanding who Jesus is, who we are as human beings and what He has done to qualify us for this precious relationship with Him. This gives us moments of pause, gratitude, awe and wonder.

This complex feeling of love, wonder and sometimes uncertainty is experienced by many who encounter the Lord Jesus in one way or another.

In the bible, Mary experienced this in her moment of surrendering to her calling to give birth the Messiah. The greeting by the angel Gabriel, took her aback.

"Gabriel appeared to her and said, "Greetings, favored woman! The Lord is with you!". Confused and disturbed, Mary tried to think what the angel could mean. "Don't be afraid, Mary," the angel told her, "for you have found favor with God! You will conceive and give birth to a son, and you will name him Jesus. He will be very great and will be called the Son of the Most High. The Lord God will give him the throne of his ancestor David. And he will reign over Israel forever; his Kingdom will never end!"
– Luke 1:28-33, New Living Translation

What a greeting and what a message! I can imagine questions flooding her mind. Gabriel's response to her reaction seemed to deal with the 'Who?', 'Me?!' and 'Why?'

questions that may have come up in her heart, which left her to ask about the 'How?'. I love that the Lord did not leave her wondering. He gives us as much of the picture as is required at certain points of our walk with Him.

Another person who could relate to Mary's amazement would be the Samaritan woman by the well with Jesus. In John 4:1-42, we see that hers was a contrary circumstance that ended with the same awe and wonder. Why would Jesus, a Jew, speak to her, a Samaritan? And, as the Messiah, how could He find her worthy of such kindness and love? He knew all about her and still offered her His living water. Everything about this moment was unheard of and frowned upon, and yet here she was receiving living water!

Peter certainly experienced this too when he met the Lord. When he realised that Jesus was the Christ, his response was to distance himself from His holiness.

When Simon Peter realized what had happened, he fell to his knees before Jesus and said, "Oh, Lord, please leave me—I'm such a sinful man." For he was awestruck by the number of fish they had caught, as were the others with him. His partners, James and John, the sons of Zebedee, were also amazed.

Jesus replied to Simon, "Don't be afraid! From now on you'll be fishing for people!" And as soon as they landed, they left everything and followed Jesus.
- Luke 5:8-11, New Living Translation

From sinful man to disciple and spiritual leader. What a transformation! I can imagine that they lived with the awe and wonder of this perfect love.

There is something about the nearness or awareness of the Lord that makes us conscious of the state of our hearts. Nothing is hidden in His presence. Truth is present in the person of Jesus, so nothing can be hidden. He sees it all and knows it all. We become fully aware that without His righteousness which is freely given to us in salvation, we are not worthy. This revelation usually stirs up repentance and alignment with the Lord.

GOD'S LOVE FOR US AND HIS PLANS FOR OUR LIVES ARE JUST AS PRECIOUS. HE DID NOT LOVE HIS FIRST DISCIPLES MORE THAN HE DOES THIS GENERATION, NEITHER ARE HIS PLANS FOR OUR LIVES LESS SIGNIFICANT THAN THEIRS.

This is something we may never fully grasp but we trust You, Lord. Please help us to receive it. Please heal and strengthen our hearts. We do not want to hear you through the filters of life's challenges, disappointments and human expectations.

Thank You Lord for choosing us and making us worthy of Your perfect love. Thank You for keeping us in Your righteousness, by the power of Your mercy and grace. May Your love continue to overwhelm and transform us. Like Mary we say:

"I am the Lord's servant. May everything you have said about me come true."
- Luke 1:38, New Living Translation

PAUSE:

Is there any truth that you struggle to receive from the Lord?

What 3 things has the Lord spoken to you in very personal ways? Bring them to mind and speak them over your life again.

Take some time to receive the love of God into your heart in a new way today.

MEDITATE:

Psalms 139:13-18 TPT

[13]You formed my innermost being, shaping my delicate inside and my intricate outside, and wove them all together in my mother's womb.

[14]I thank you, God, for making me so mysteriously complex!
Everything you do is marvelously breathtaking.
It simply amazes me to think about it!
How thoroughly you know me, Lord!

[15]You even formed every bone in my body when you created me in the secret place; carefully, skillfully you shaped me from nothing to something.

[16]You saw who you created me to be before I became me!
Before I'd ever seen the light of day, the number of days you planned for me were already recorded in your book.

[17-18]Every single moment you are thinking of me!
How precious and wonderful to consider that you cherish me constantly in your every thought!
O God, your desires toward me are more than the grains of sand on every shore!
When I awake each morning, you're still with me.

NO! NOT ME!

11
NO! NOT ME!

You did not take it from me
It is rightfully yours
I don't know why I'm envious
I'm not sure why I fuss

I really should celebrate
Your good news with you
but I am having a hard time
and wondering what to do

Clearly I've been competing
I didn't know it was with you
Your success is not my failure
we all know this is true

Something is really wrong, Lord
and It's happening in my heart
Please heal whatever is broken
and help me with a new start

There are sins that are appealing because they seem to be fun and some that seem reasonable because we can explain them away. There are some sins that are universally condemned as pure evil and there are some that are shameful and bring disgrace.

However, there are two that are at the root of so much evil.

They are only seen by the damaging and sabotaging fruit that they produce through the words and actions of anyone who is under their influence. They are conceived and nurtured in the hiddenness of the heart, and gain power and control by remaining undetected.

I believe that a lot of Christians would easily confess to other sins than these because of the pride that masks the shame they thrive in.

Meet Jealousy and Envy. The spiritually poisonous twins of the unrenewed mind!

I AM NOT CLAIMING THAT THESE TWO ARE WORSE THAN ANY OTHER SINS. EVERY ACT OF SIN IS UNACCEPTABLE TO THE LORD. HE HATES SIN BECAUSE IT IS DIRECTLY OPPOSED TO HIS NATURE AND ALL THAT HE STANDS FOR.

This is why He dealt with the nature of sin in creation by Jesus's sacrifice. The Holy God became man to overcome the sin nature by becoming it. He did not sin once but took on the sin nature and all of its expressions into Himself, so it would die with Him and satisfy its ultimate power which is death. His resurrection put it in the past as a dead issue and turned a new page for creation. He restored spiritual order and crushed the devil's claims of dominion, power and authority over creation.

The Lord Jesus redeemed us into His holy nature through our salvation. We are 'Born Again'! No longer just born by human flesh but born by the Holy Spirt of God. Our nature has been changed.

Jealousy and envy are no longer a part of our character. It is now unnatural for us to think or wish evil on others. This is not a part of our holy nature. They can only survive in hearts that do not know, or have forgotten who they truly are.

There is something about comparing ourselves with oth-ers, maliciously wanting what they have, or scheming ways to sabotage their progress because of our insecurity; that requires a deep sense of personal insignificance.

This might also be why it is often denied or ignored by many. Although it is a shameful act, denying its operation in our hearts is not the solution.

Can you tell when it is envy or jealousy, not something wrong with the other person?

Jealousy and envy are fueled by an unhealthy need for personal success or completeness.

They thrive in our hearts when we:

- want what others have and are not happy that they have it.

- suddenly feel uncomfortable and incomplete because of someone else's good news.

- are not content with our own lives and want what others have, without their personal process or sacrifices.

- have godly desires but are not willing to wait our turn.

- question the Lord's plan, wisdom and timing for our lives.

- are in competition with everyone because we always want to be ahead.

What starts as a feeling in a moment, becomes a seed that takes root and over time influences our desires, perceptions, thoughts and motives.

There is no universal measurement for success, except for what has been portrayed by worldly standards. Success is different from person to person because only our creator can confirm whether or not we are successful in light of His plans for our individual lives.

The world considers us to be successful when we do well with our health, finances, relationships, careers and lifestyle.

In the Lord's ways, success for one person could be failure for another person. He measures it very differently. The fruit of our spiritual lives matter more than the fruit of our pursuits and labours.

Here is a reminder of the standard that He set for us as His people, with His holy nature:

"The behavior of the self-life is obvious: Sexual immorality, lustful thoughts, pornography, chasing after things instead of God, manipulating others, hatred of those who get in your way, senseless arguments, resentment when others are favored, temper tantrums, angry quarrels, only thinking of yourself, being in love with your own opinions, being envious of the blessings of others, murder, uncontrolled addictions, wild parties, and all other similar behavior.

Haven't I already warned you that those who use their "freedom" for these things will not inherit the kingdom realm of God! But the fruit produced by the Holy Spirit within you is divine love in all its varied expressions: joy that overflows, peace that subdues, patience that endures, kindness in action, a life full of virtue, faith that prevails, gentleness of heart, and strength of spirit. Never set the law above these qualities, for they are meant to be limitless."
- Galatians 5:19-23 TPT

The fruit of the spirit and our obedience to the Lord's plans for our lives is our measure of success.

You may be wondering: If jealousy is so bad then why would the bible say God is a jealous God?

Our heavenly Father's jealousy is pure. His jealousy is a response to our rebellion and an expression of His unchanging love for us.

In the context of our rebellion, we were created for great and wonderful purposes, according to His plan. So, God's jealousy is an expression of anger at the sin and path of destruction we are set on. His jealousy moves to destroy whatever stands in the way of our connection with us and realigns us with His plan.

He made us for Himself and gave us the authority to represent Him, with the freewill to choose oneness with Him. He longs for us to be in close fellowship and partnership with Him, as He designed. His jealousy for us protects and corrects us at the same time.

Our jealousy and envy comes from an evil place. God cannot envy. He is everything and is lacking nothing. He does not want what we have. Every good and perfect gift comes from Him, according to James 1:17. He made us the wonderful beings that we are. He just wants us in deep communion with Him and wants us to want Him by choice.

PAUSE:

How have you dealt with the temptation to envy or become jealous of others?

Here is a practical tip for dealing with envy and jealousy in your relationships.

- Catch the thought. It always starts with a thought.

- Identify its purpose. (The thief comes only in order to steal and kill and destroy. - John 10:10 Amplified Bible)

- Reject it by refusing what it is offering. It would usually be: offence, suspicion, competition, strife and shame.

- Call it by its name and cast it out of your heart.

- Kill it off by speaking a blessing over the person instead.

- Affirm your heart and identity with God's truth about you.

MEDITATE:

James 4:1-3, New Living Translation
4 What is causing the quarrels and fights among you? Don't they come from the evil desires at war within you? [2] You want what you don't have, so you scheme and kill to get it. You are jealous of what others have, but you can't get it, so you fight and wage war to take it away from them. Yet you don't have what you want because you don't ask God for it. [3] And even when you ask, you don't get it because your motives are all wrong—you want only what will give you pleasure.

John 3:3-8, New Living Translation
[3] Jesus replied, "I tell you the truth, unless you are born again, you cannot see the Kingdom of God."

[4] "What do you mean?" exclaimed Nicodemus. "How can an old man go back into his mother's womb and be born again?"

[5] Jesus replied, "I assure you, no one can enter the Kingdom of God without being born of water and the Spirit. [6] Humans can reproduce only human life, but the Holy Spirit gives birth to spiritual life. [7] So don't be surprised when I say, 'You must be born again.' [8] The wind blows wherever it wants. Just as you can hear the wind but can't tell where it comes from or where it is going, so you can't explain how people are born of the Spirit."

James 3:14-17, New Living Translation

[14] But if you are bitterly jealous and there is selfish ambition in your heart, don't cover up the truth with boasting and lying. [15] For jealousy and selfishness are not God's kind of wisdom. Such things are earthly, unspiritual, and demonic. [16] For wherever there is jealousy and selfish ambition, there you will find disorder and evil of every kind.

[17] But the wisdom from above is first of all pure. It is also peace loving, gentle at all times, and willing to yield to others. It is full of mercy and the fruit of good deeds. It shows no favoritism and is always sincere.

YOUR PEACE, MY PEACE

12
YOUR PEACE, MY PEACE

The peace that you have given
so lavishly to me
It did not cost me anything
but for You it was not free

You died so I would have it
to live life full and free
It is my precious treasure
and forever it will be

I do my best to keep it
it'll cost too much to lose
A life of inner harmony
is what I daily choose

No one can match the price
or make a good enough offer
Your peace is mine, I rest in this
so shall it be forever

True peace is a precious thing. It is an inner stillness and stability that we experience irrespective of our external environments.

It cannot be attained by controlling everything that happens to us or around us, but it is received as a gift and maintained by regulating what happens in our hearts.

As children of God, our peace is a gift from our Lord Jesus Christ. He gave His life to get it to us and it can never be taken away. It might sound impossible to never lose your peace, but it is true. We actually never lose our peace. We lose our awareness of it.

When our attention is captured by disturbances, it may seem like our peace is gone. However all we are experiencing is external activity that is impacting us physically and emotionally. This still does not mean our peace is gone. Even in the most turbulent seasons of our lives, our peace is still intact. Our emotions may be all over the place, but our peace is still completely in place.

So why do we get so troubled and afraid? Could it be because we have forgotten about the peace that we were given?

"Peace I leave with you; My [perfect] peace I give to you; not as the world gives do I give to you. Do not let your heart be troubled, nor let it be afraid. [Let My perfect peace calm you in every circumstance and give you courage and strength for every challenge.]"
- John 14:27, Amplified Bible

The Lord did not just give us His peace but He also told us how to maintain it as our reality. In that verse of scripture there are two clear instructions for maintaining a heart posture of peace:

1. Do not let your heart be troubled,

2. Nor let it be afraid.

How do you not get troubled in troubling situations?
How do you not get afraid in fearful circumstances?

It is all about your focus. What are you focusing on in those times? There is no denying whatever you maybe experiencing, but is that all you see?

Have you forgotten about your Lord?
Have you forgotten that He is with you even then?
Have you lost every sense of His greatness over your situation?
Have you forgotten His peace is your peace too?

The Lord is not without empathy and compassion towards us. He feels our pain and sees our struggle but He is not troubled by any of it. Yes, He sees the bigger picture and knows just how to work it all out. That is why the best thing to do is to embrace His peace about it. Not because you can see the end of it or understand His ways, but because You trust Him. You remember His word and His promises. You know that even in the bleakest of circumstances He still makes a way. Even in times of great sorrow and loss, He is right there with you.

Our instruction is to 'not let' which means to 'not allow'.
Do not allow yourself to be troubled.
Do not allow yourself to be afraid.

Trouble will come and fear will come, but you should not give in to them and let them rule your heart. Remembering that the Lord is always with you and focusing on His truth concerning you, is how to not be troubled or afraid.

"You will guard him *and* keep him in perfect *and*
constant peace whose mind [both its inclination and its
character] is stayed on You, because he commits himself
to You, leans on You, *and* hopes confidently in You."
- Isaiah 26:3, Amplified Bible Classic Edition

THIS PEACE IS AN IRREVOCABLE GIFT TO US. WE NEVER LOSE IT. WE MAY LOSE OUR AWARENESS OF IT, BUT WE NEVER LOSE IT. TO LOSE OUR PEACE IS TO BE TOTALLY DISCONNECTED FROM THE PRINCE OF PEACE HIMSELF.

Peace is not a feeling or a mood. Peace is the stillness and stability that comes from the understanding of the Lord's unfailing love for us. To know Jesus personally, is to know peace deeply.

We sometimes give our peace away too easily. It costs too much to be stolen without a fight.

PAUSE:

Are you able to identify the easiest ways that your awareness of peace is disrupted?

How well do you guard your heart to protect your peace?

Be more intentional about staying aware of the Lord's presence with you. How can you practice this?

How can you help others to engage with God's peace?

MEDITATE:

Proverbs 4:23 TPT
So above all, guard the affections of your heart, for they affect all that you are. Pay attention to the welfare of your innermost being, for from there flows the wellspring of life.

Philippians 4:6-8, New Living Translation
[6] Don't worry about anything; instead, pray about everything. Tell God what you need, and thank him for all he has done. [7] Then you will experience God's peace, which exceeds anything we can understand. His peace will guard your hearts and minds as you live in Christ Jesus.

[8] And now, dear brothers and sisters, one final thing. Fix your thoughts on what is true, and honorable, and right, and pure, and lovely, and admirable. Think about things that are excellent and worthy of praise.

Matthew 6:25-33, New Living Translation
[25] "That is why I tell you not to worry about everyday life—whether you have enough food and drink, or enough clothes to wear. Isn't life more than food, and your body more than clothing? [26] Look at the birds. They don't plant or harvest or store food in barns, for your heavenly Father feeds them. And aren't you far more valuable to him than they are? [27] Can all your worries add a single moment to your life?

[28] "And why worry about your clothing? Look at the lilies of the field and how they grow. They don't work or make their clothing, [29] yet Solomon in all his glory was not dressed as beautifully as they are. [30] And if God cares so wonderfully for wildflowers that are here today and thrown into the fire tomorrow, he will certainly care for you. Why do you have so little faith?

[31] "So don't worry about these things, saying, 'What will we eat? What will we drink? What will we wear?' [32] These things dominate the thoughts of unbelievers, but your heavenly Father already knows all your needs. [33] Seek the Kingdom of God above all else, and live righteously, and he will give you everything you need.

Colossians 3:15 TPT
Let your heart be always guided by the peace of the Anointed One, who called you to peace as part of his one body. And always be thankful.

MY GOD ENCOUNTER

13
MY GOD ENCOUNTER

They say that you're a healer
that you can set me free
They say that you have given
back our full authority

I've heard so many stories
and seen some of the proof
For fear of disappointment
I still remained aloof

It's clear that you can do it
but will You do it for me?
I have never been chosen
or made a priority

I really want to experience
Your presence in this place
Please Lord help me to receive
Your goodness, power and grace

To help stir up my faith
please tell me your experience
How was your own encounter?
What was it like in His Presence?

- Me (The expectant one - Here and now)

Looking through the scriptures and wanting to encourage
your heart, here are some responses that I imagined you
might get:

I had heard more than enough
I could not wait any longer
I decided that my turn had come
My faith had only grown stronger

I hoped to get close enough
To reach Him through the crowd
It helped that no one saw me
It helped that they were loud

My heart was gripped with fear
My body was weak and frail
This was my final hope
I couldn't afford to fail

I didn't need to be acknowledged
I needed to be healed
and with one touch of His garment
that desire was fulfilled.

**- Beloved Daughter (aka. Woman with the issue of blood
- Matthew 9:20-22)**

I heard all of the noise
the footsteps got louder
He was surely walking by
this made me so much bolder

I didn't have much to lose
all I had was my shame
I refused to be silent
I refused to remain the same

This was my day of promise
My promise to myself
That one day I would meet Him
and stand amongst the twelve

I raised my voice and called out
appealing to His Grace
He spoke the words I needed
and helped me see to His face

- Bartimaeus (Once Blind - Luke 18:35-43)

I knew that I was hated
but I had to take my chance
He was right there in our midst
but I couldn't catch a glance

I may never come this close again
to seeing this holy Teacher
The Messiah, as some called Him
He was also called a healer

I wanted to speak with Him
but others were in the way
His loving nature drew me in
and with Him I wanted to stay

I found a way to see Him
without a push or shove
He called me down and followed me home
Mine was an encounter of redemptive love

- Zacchaeus (less hated Tax Collector - Luke 19:1-10

It was the craziest idea
but it was worth the try
Those determined friends of mine
would not leave me to die

I had suffered for so long
always feeling like a burden.
Watching others get on with life
while I felt like a weed in a garden

I was very much concerned
about the damage to the roof
but they said it would be worth it
and my healing was the proof

He had to pause His sermon
And give in to their faith
He forgave my sins and healed me
Since then life has been great!

- Healed and Forgiven (aka. Paralyzed man with the faithful friends - Luke 5:17-26)

How did it all happen?
I can't fully explain
Something happened inside me
when He called me by my name.

The torment was now over
my sins were washed away
I was made free to go and live
but with Him I chose to stay

He became my Lord and Master
My Messiah and my Friend
The only one I live for
The one I would defend

He spoke of resurrection
still we were unprepared
I am grateful to have been there
This good news was to be shared

- Mary Magdalene (Friend of Jesus - John 20:11-18)

These people were intentional about engaging with the Lord. They all had different needs and received from Him in different ways.

WE ARE NEVER TOO FAR, TOO HIDDEN, TOO REJECTED OR TOO DAMAGED TO BE TRANSFORMED BY OUR SAVIOUR'S LOVE.

Make this moment your own with Him. He knows you, He sees you, He cares for you and He is waiting for you.

PAUSE:

Holy Spirit is God. He is not a feeling you get to confirm the Lord's presence. He is also not an event. Take a moment to be aware of His presence with you, right now.

Yield your heart to the Lord by faith in His word, which is truth.

Which scripture are you connecting your faith to right now?

Go ahead and share your heart with the Lord.

What is He saying to you?

MEDITATE:

John 16:12-14, Amplified Bible, Classic Edition

[12] I have still many things to say to you, but you are not able to bear them *or* to take them upon you *or* to grasp them now.

[13] But when He, the Spirit of Truth (the Truth-giving Spirit) comes, He will guide you into all the Truth (the whole, full Truth). For He will not speak His own message [on His own authority]; but He will tell whatever He hears [from the Father; He will give the message that has been given to Him], and He will announce *and* declare to you the things that are to come [that will happen in the future].

[14] He will honor *and* glorify Me, because He will take of (receive, draw upon) what is Mine and will reveal (declare, disclose, transmit) it to you.

John 10:27-30, New Living Translation

[27] My sheep listen to my voice; I know them, and they follow me. [28] I give them eternal life, and they will never perish. No one can snatch them away from me, [29] for my Father has given them to me, and he is more powerful than anyone else. No one can snatch them from the Father's hand. [30] The Father and I are one."

John 14:26, Amplified Bible
But the Helper (Comforter, Advocate, Intercessor—Counselor, Strengthener, Standby), the Holy Spirit, whom the Father will send in My name [in My place, to represent Me and act on My behalf], He will teach you all things. And He will help you remember everything that I have told you.

ABIDE AND BE

14
ABIDE AND BE

I still cannot believe
what is happening to me
I wake up so joyful
I walk around carefree

I could not remember
when last I had a laugh
but here I am telling jokes
amusing all the staff

I know that they are wondering
what happened to the grouch
who refused to be friendly
and walked with a slouch

This isn't just an outward thing
it is happening deep inside
Something in me has come alive
Something I thought had died

I am a testimony
There's so much to be shared
This joy is overwhelming
It is way over my head

This is the love of Jesus
an encounter with His grace
and basking in His presence
is now my happy place!

'People can change'. This statement would easily spark a debate which would support the opposing view that humans are flawed creatures that lack the ability to truly change in character.

Apostle Paul would be a great example of such a transformation. The one who once persecuted followers of Jesus, became His committed disciple and servant. His transformation was so incredible that he needed Barnabas to vouch for him before the other apostles.[2]

Moses was also one who publicly switched sides. He was known to serve Egyptian gods, as one raised in Pharaoh's household. Years later, he returned as a messenger of 'I Am', sent back to God's people, who actually were his people too. His claim of having encountered their God required proof, hence the signs that the Lord had given to him. The signs and plagues were just as much a confirmation for the Israelites, as they were for the Egyptians.[3]

The Samaritan woman by the well is another example of a powerfully transformed life. She went to the well as an unbelieving Samaritan known for her shameful circumstances, but returned as a joyful woman proclaiming Jesus as the Messiah. Her transformation was so compelling that they had to come and see Him for themselves.[4]

---

[2] Acts 9:26-28
[3] Exodus 4:1-9
[4] Exodus 4:1-9

When I look back at my life, I am grateful to see how far the Lord has brought me. He has changed my life completely. He took me from where I was and set me on this path of newness, restoration, character development, intimacy with Him and purpose fulfilment. It remains a progressive walk of growth and oneness with Him.

The deeper you grow in intimacy with the Lord, the more you enjoy the benefits of being in His Presence. According to the scriptures, 'without Him we can do nothing' [5] and 'in His presence is fullness of joy and pleasures for evermore' [6]. His presence is our safe place of growth, joy and fulfilment.

"You are the light of [Christ to] the world. A city set on a hill cannot be hidden; nor does *anyone* light a lamp and put it under a basket, but on a lampstand, and it gives light to all who are in the house. Let your light shine before men in such a way that they may see your good deeds *and* moral excellence, and [recognize and honor and] glorify your Father who is in heaven.
- Matthew 5:14-16, Amplified Bible

LETTING OUR LIGHT SHINE IS NOT ALL ABOUT TALKING TO PEOPLE ABOUT JESUS, IT IS ALSO ABOUT THEM SEEING HIM IN US. THIS EVIDENCE WOULD BE SEEN IN EVERY AREA OF OUR LIVES; IN OUR VALUES, COMMUNICATION, ATTITUDES, COMMITMENTS AND ACTIONS.

---

[5] John 15:5
[6] Psalm 16:11

Jesus is not hidden in our hearts, He is alive in us. The fruit of His Spirit's influence on our spirit cannot be hidden. Neither can we keep our hearts hidden from the Lord.

"Behold, I stand at the door [of the church] and *continually* knock. If anyone hears My voice and opens the door, I will come in and eat with him (restore him), and he with Me."
- Revelation 3:20, Amplified Bible

This verse which was written to the church in Laodicea, also applies to us as individual members of the Body of Christ. He is continually knocking on the doors of our hearts, seeking deeper fellowship with us.

He is still knocking and drawing your attention to the parts of your life that He needs to be invited into. Can you hear it? Can you feel it? Are you willing to let Him in?

There is always going to be a part of your heart that needs His touch. Let Him in deeper today, so that you may experience another level of freedom and fullness. Also, so that others may enjoy more of Him through your interactions with them.

PAUSE:

Are people experiencing Jesus through you?

What would it look like for the Light of God to shine brightly through you?

Is there any area of your life that you need the Lord to touch, restore or transform? He is able and willing. Invite Him in.

MEDITATE:

2 Corinthians 5:17, Amplified Bible
Therefore if anyone is in Christ [that is, grafted in, joined to Him by faith in Him as Savior], *he is* a new creature [reborn and renewed by the Holy Spirit]; the old things [the previous moral and spiritual condition] have passed away. Behold, new things have come [because spiritual awakening brings a new life].

Romans 10:9-10, Amplified Bible
[9]because if you acknowledge *and* confess with your mouth that Jesus is Lord [recognizing His power, authority, and majesty as God], and believe in your heart that God raised Him from the dead, you will be saved. [10] For with the heart a person believes [in Christ as Savior] resulting in his justification [that is, being made righteous—being freed of the guilt of sin and made acceptable to God]; and with the mouth he acknowledges *and* confesses [his faith openly], resulting in *and* confirming [his] salvation.

Ephesians 2:8-10, New Living Translation
[8] God saved you by his grace when you believed. And you can't take credit for this; it is a gift from God. [9] Salvation is not a reward for the good things we have done, so none of us can boast about it. [10] For we are God's masterpiece. He has created us anew in Christ Jesus, so we can do the good things he planned for us long ago.

THE PRICE OF ACCEPTANCE

15
THE PRICE OF ACCEPTANCE

They like it when I'm not myself
though they don't know who I am
I have taken on a personality
that presents as really calm

I am actually very chatty
I am bubbly and I'm loud
and when I'm really happy
I stand out in a crowd

Sometimes I can't remember
the things I truly enjoy
I've done so much to fit in
I've fallen for the ploy

It's sad that those around me
believe this 'me' they see
The idea that I could be different
is not even a possibility

I guess I cannot blame them
The fault is all my own
because I keep pretending
afraid of being known

I wonder why I do this
When did it really start?
Was it when I was bullied
and told I was not smart?

My sad need for acceptance
has led me down this path
The real cost of this detour
is way beyond my math

The way that I've been living
is denying my own birth
The time has come to be myself
Here I am. Hello earth!

Some popular false claims:

"I know myself."
"This is just how I am."
"I have always been like this."
"I don't care what anybody thinks!"
"No one gets me."
" Everybody loves me!"

When we say 'we know ourselves', what we typically mean is that we know our preferences, aversions, habits, experiences, abilities, limitations, past choices, tendencies, family history, personal dreams, goals, cares and fears. We learn these as we grow and participate in daily life. What we claim to know about ourselves is usually what we have experienced or been exposed to so far.

Who we are is so much more than what we have done or experienced in life. Although all of the above are a part of life's journey, they do not inform us of our identity.

Our identity and purpose as human beings are found in our relationship with God, through the Lord Jesus Christ. Embracing this relationship introduces us to our true nature, purpose and abilities. This in turn helps to guide our words, thoughts and actions; which helps to form our values, character, habits and preferences. All of which influence our choices.

Choices tend to be made based on our feelings, as opposed to our true identity. This is common because a lot of people believe that their identity is based on how they feel. Our feelings change so often that being led by them makes one unstable in character. Adopting whichever personality benefits us and holding fast to lies in place of the truth is very confusing for the human soul, which naturally draws on whatever it experiences. Our soul comprises of our mind, will, emotions, intellect and imagination. Without the filter of Truth, the Word and Spirit of God, the human soul is left in a state of utter confusion. As the bible states, "God is not the author of confusion" [7].

THERE IS A STORY LONG AGO WRITTEN AND YET UNTOLD. THE TELLING OF THIS STORY IS DONE DAY BY DAY AS EACH ASPECT PLAYS OUT THROUGH THE LIFE OF ITS MAIN CHARACTER.

I am speaking about your God-written story. The detailed and wonderful collection of His thoughts, plans, goals, dreams, gifts, opportunities, assignments, relationships, privileges, victories and blessings; that weave together to make up the scroll of destiny that only you can fulfil.

You were created to give a unique expression of all you were prepared for. You are not meant to be in competition with anyone else and you are definitely not meant to live in comparison to anyone else either.

---

[7] 1 Corinthians 14:33

Know that not everyone will get you or like what you have to offer. That is acceptable because we all have a right to our preferences. Just make sure that you do not take it to heart as rejection and nurture it as a wound. We are all someone's preference. The concept of uniqueness and diversity allows for there to be options and differences of opinion.

If no one ever disagrees with you, then someone is lying to you. Think about it, you don't agree with everyone else too.

The world is waiting to be blessed by you. Yes, you!

Come forth!

PAUSE:

Take a moment to ask yourself these questions:

Whose life am I living?

Am I living in fear of failure and ignoring the gifts and talents that I have been blessed with?

Am I living a life dictated by my conveniences, thereby forgoing growth opportunities?

Have I given up displaying Christ-like character for fear of rejection?

Is my God-written story being told, or am I telling my preferred version?

Will others ever get to know who I really am, as the Lord intended?

Make sure you say a prayer of repentance when you are convicted in your heart about the truth.

Position your heart to accept God's loving truth about you and ask for the grace to receive it. He finds you worthy.

Is there any corresponding action you should take?

MEDITATE:

Psalm 139:16, New Living Translation
¹⁶ You saw me before I was born. Every day of my life was recorded in your book. Every moment was laid out before a single day had passed.

Jeremiah 29:11-13, New Living Translation
¹¹ For I know the plans I have for you," says the LORD. "They are plans for good and not for disaster, to give you a future and a hope. ¹² In those days when you pray, I will listen. ¹³ If you look for me wholeheartedly, you will find me.

Luke 6:26-30, The Message
²⁶ "There's trouble ahead when you live only for the approval of others, saying what flatters them, doing what indulges them. Popularity contests are not truth contests—look how many scoundrel preachers were approved by your ancestors! Your task is to be true, not popular.

²⁷⁻³⁰ "To you who are ready for the truth, I say this: Love your enemies. Let them bring out the best in you, not the worst. When someone gives you a hard time, respond with the supple moves of prayer for that person. If someone slaps you in the face, stand there and take it. If someone grabs your

shirt, giftwrap your best coat and make a present of it. If someone takes unfair advantage of you, use the occasion to practice the servant life. No more payback. Live generously.

YOURS SINCERELY

16
YOURS SINCERELY

You began this journey with Me
not sure how it would go
You had wrong ways of thinking
and issues that didn't show

You trusted in My nature
that does not heap on shame
Each time was very different
and now you are not the same

This is a lifetime process
of walking in My ways
It will take your commitment
to do this all of your days

In your moments of weakness
come boldly to My throne
Know that I am always with you
In Me you've found a home

You laid your heart before Me
your sins you did not hide
My love and truth have healed you
and made you new inside

In your own way you gave me
what you called your whole heart
With love and joy, I say to you
Now, here is your whole heart

PAUSE:

Take a moment to receive that from the Lord's heart to yours.

What does this mean to you?

How can you apply this word of affirmation in your life?

Revisit this place of affirmation often.

MEDITATE:

Proverbs 3:1-10, New Living Translation
My child, never forget the things I have taught you.
 Store my commands in your heart.
² If you do this, you will live many years,
 and your life will be satisfying.
³ Never let loyalty and kindness leave you!
 Tie them around your neck as a reminder.
 Write them deep within your heart.
⁴ Then you will find favor with both God and people,
 and you will earn a good reputation.

⁵ Trust in the LORD with all your heart;
 do not depend on your own understanding.
⁶ Seek his will in all you do,
 and he will show you which path to take.

⁷ Don't be impressed with your own wisdom.
 Instead, fear the LORD and turn away from evil.
⁸ Then you will have healing for your body
 and strength for your bones.

⁹ Honor the LORD with your wealth
 and with the best part of everything you produce.
¹⁰ Then he will fill your barns with grain,
 and your vats will overflow with good wine.

James 1:22-25, New Living Translation

[22] But don't just listen to God's word. You must do what it says. Otherwise, you are only fooling yourselves. [23] For if you listen to the word and don't obey, it is like glancing at your face in a mirror. [24] You see yourself, walk away, and forget what you look like. [25] But if you look carefully into the perfect law that sets you free, and if you do what it says and don't forget what you heard, then God will bless you for doing it.

YOUR HEART'S RESPONSE

17
YOUR HEART'S RESPONSE

My heart is beating quickly
It's not the usual rhythm
I feel like I have been on
a rollercoaster ride from heaven

Sometimes I felt delighted
Sometimes I felt upset
You walked me down this narrow path
to help me hit reset

It really is amazing
to find the things we hide
The fear, the shame, the pretence
the guilt, the pain, the pride

Thank You for the invitation
and for showing me myself
For teaching and restoring me
to Your truth and nothing else

Help me always remember
just how much I am loved
You have given so lavishly
I really feel quite chuffed

This is a new beginning
of walking in Your ways
You are my heart's desire
My Lord, You have my praise!

MY PRAYER FOR YOU

18
MY PRAYER FOR YOU

On the days that you are happy
On the days that you are sad
On the days that you are hopeful
and the days that you are glad

In the times of difficulty
In those moments of despair
When you are feeling lonely
and there is no one there

In times of great excitement
when you do not have a care
While waiting in expectation
for that great news to share

Know that the Lord is with you
He is always right there
You are His special treasure
His heart with you He'll share

No matter what may happen
He will not let you down
His plans may be much different
from what you're thinking now

He knows just how to love you
to heal you and to guide
He is forever faithful
and He will never leave your side

Shalom
Shalom

ABOUT THE AUTHOR

Valerie Eme Elyott is a woman with a passion for seeing people mature in their walk with God and maintain an intimate relationship with Him. She supports people in their journey of spiritual growth and hosts gatherings to facilitate the same.

She is the founder of The Elyott Generation, a multigenerational ministry that inspires intimacy with the Lord and equips people to walk in their callings.

For more information visit www.valeriee.online.